Original title:
A Philosophical Approach to Finding the Remote

Copyright © 2025 Creative Arts Management OÜ
All rights reserved.

Author: George Mercer
ISBN HARDBACK: 978-1-80566-071-2
ISBN PAPERBACK: 978-1-80566-366-9

The Quest Beneath the Surface

In the couch's depths, a treasure hides,
Beneath the cushions, chaos abides.
I probe with fingers, a daring quest,
For the elusive button, oh what a test!

A rogue snack wrapper, I must confront,
What a strange world, my couch is a front!
Remote control? I laugh and I groan,
It feels like searching for a lost bone!

Under coffee mugs, and heaps of fluff,
Why is this journey always so tough?
I find old coins, and a wayward sock,
But that remote's hidden behind the clock!

Fellow couch potatoes, I call to you,
We unite in this scavenger stew!
With laughter we share, and tales of our woe,
One day we'll triumph, with tacos in tow!

The Threshold of Comfort

In the couch's embrace, I sink deep,
Lost amidst cushions, my soul starts to creep.
The remote, that elusive, tiny device,
Tucked in between, oh, isn't it nice?

I check under pillows, I check in the dark,
Searching for answers, I leave quite a mark.
Hours may drift, with snacks left to spoil,
But this quest for my channel brings tears of toil.

An Odyssey of Overlooked Identifiers

A quest of confusion, a map made of fluff,
Identifying buttons is getting quite tough.
The 'power' feels weak as I press it in rage,
Yet comfort remains locked in a digital cage.

The dog gives me looks like I'm losing my mind,
As I sift through the clutter, unorthodox grime.
Each swipe of the hand spurs new misadventures,
In the land of the lazy, I've lost all my tensions.

Seeking Stillness in a World of Movement

Once a sleek remote, now a ghost in the fray,
Vibes full of action, they lead me astray.
The suspense thickens, where did it go?
A martial arts move brings out the inner pro.

The TV taunts me with its glowing blue eye,
While I ponder existence and just wonder why.
This search is profound, like life's great debate,
Remote, where are you? Let's sync up our fate.

The Pathway to the Perfect Channel

Amidst all the chaos, treasures await,
With a bowl full of popcorn, oh, isn't it great?
Fumbling through cushions like treasures of old,
The stories unfolding, like fortunes foretold.

At last, I discover my silver remote,
It was here all along, like a trustworthy note.
Now, I may sit back and let laughter ensue,
For the pathway to channels was seeking me too.

The Hidden Tapestry of Connectivity

In cushions deep, the secrets lie,
The echo of laughter, a distant sigh.
Among the socks and crumbs we chase,
A world of buttons, a hidden place.

The dog sits proud, guarding his spot,
While I'm on my quest, giving it thought.
Remote controls, like dreams that float,
Hide in plain sight, on the couch they gloat.

Understanding Life's Channels

Flipping through lives that never seem real,
Each click a chance, for joy we feel.
Friends through screens, oh so divine,
But where is my remote? Somewhere it shined!

Docu-series on life's grand quest,
Yet the remote is lost, what a jest!
A chase through the kitchen, a run by the door,
In this game of hide and seek, who could want more?

Between Comfort and Complacency

Nestled in blankets, feeling so fine,
While exploring the channels, one at a time.
Oh, the quest is fun, though at times it's bleak,
For every good movie, there's a dull peak.

But here I lie, my snacks piled high,
Remote control hunting? Oh me, oh my!
A cup of joy, a slice of doubt,
What will I watch, when I figure it out?

Navigating the Seas of Choices

A map of options, a flicker of light,
To dive into joy, or choose a fright.
Each button's a treasure, each channel a tale,
Yet the remote eludes me like a ship with a sail.

With laughter and snacks, I try to decide,
Navigate this maze, with friends by my side.
In the sea of decisions, I'll take the dive,
Finding the remote, oh how I strive!

The Remote Control of Thought

In a couch of clouds I sit,
Grabbing dreams, a mental fit.
Channels change with every blink,
But where's the control? I think.

Thoughts are scattered like lost socks,
Searching for the hidden clocks.
Between the cushions lies my fate,
A quest that's never, ever late.

In Pursuit of the Elusive Click

A button here, a button there,
I seek the remote with great despair.
It's hiding like a ninja sly,
I wonder if it's learned to fly.

I pound the cushions, sift the fluff,
This journey here can get quite tough.
Yet in the search, there's joy to find,
A tangled quest, with laughs entwined.

Tuning Into the Silence

With every button pressed, I sigh,
  The air is thick as I comply.
Beneath the static, whispers spark,
  In silence lurks a comedic arc.

I find the volume—up and down,
The TV grins, the silence frowns.
A cosmic joke, I must decode,
While shushing dreams like they're on load.

The Philosophy Behind the Pause

In pause, I ponder deep and wide,
What choices made the pixels slide?
Each moment's like a movie scene,
With bloopers hidden in between.

A fleeting thought, a fleeting grin,
The 'play' returns; let chaos begin!
With every press, I juggle fate,
This dance of life is never late.

The Gratification of a Single Press

A button pressed, with utmost glee,
Who knew such power lived in me?
To flick a switch, oh what a thrill,
Yet every channel, still I fill.

I search for joy in static drones,
With every click, I find new zones.
The prize is clear, a laugh or two,
To switch it up, what else to do?

Existential Questions in Flipping Through Life

What is the meaning, a channel to chase?
As I navigate this viewing space.
Life flickers by in hues of absurd,
Is Netflix my fate, or just a word?

I ponder deeply, remote in hand,
Like a philosopher lost in TV land.
Do I seek less drama or more rerun?
Each choice I make feels like a pun.

Moments Lost Between Scenes

Life's a show, yet I miss the plot,
Flipping through moments, oh what a lot!
Commercial breaks steal precious time,
The laughter fades, oh how I pine.

Rewind the joy, fast-forward regret,
In between scenes, memories unset.
Grab the popcorn; savor the taste,
Each missed moment, a comical waste.

Mediations of the Absence

Alone with the remote, a chance to reflect,
Is it me or the couch that's become an object?
I summon the shows, like spirits at play,
Yet disconnect lingers, what can I say?

Absence of friends, replaced by a screen,
In laughter and silence, I'm stuck in between.
The comedy flows; I sip on my grief,
Finding solace in joy, is that disbelief?

The Space Between Shows

In the couch's deep embrace, we seek,
Lost in cushions, we dare to peek.
The remote, a phantom, slips away,
Like time, it hides, refusing to play.

We search like treasure hunters bold,
In the realm of snacks and stories untold.
What's the point of bingeing our faves,
If finding the tool gets us lost like knaves?

Existential Navigation in the Living Room

Where did it go, the magical wand?
Is it under the dog, or lost in the beyond?
Do we control the screen, or does it control us?
In this cosmic dance, we express our fuss.

Remote lost in its maze of a couch,
Philosophers debate; we just slouch.
Is the journey enlightening, or just plain lame?
In this quest, I'm still searching for the name.

The Paradox of Effortless Convenience

With a button, we alter reality's flow,
Yet behind that ease, a struggle can grow.
Oh, the irony of progress gone wrong,
In seeking leisure, we don't quite belong.

Convenience gleams, but chaos unfolds,
Like socks mismatched, our patience behold.
As the episode starts and the credits roll,
I find my remote—oh, the toll on my soul!

Signals Sent and Emotions Caught

I wave my arms; it doesn't respond,
Is it me, or is it just beyond?
Signals cross in this silly strife,
Each press a gamble, a game of life.

Emotions rollercoaster but no show in sight,
We laugh at the absurdity; what a hilarious plight!
In the search for pleasure, we often forget,
The remote's just a remnant of every regret.

Signals in the Static

In the couch, I sit and see,
What's that buzzing? Is it me?
I lift the cushions, dive so deep,
Will I find it, or lose sleep?

Lost within the channels flow,
Footprints lead where I don't know.
The static crackles, hints and teases,
Remote control is lost with ease.

A bold adventure, couch explorin',
Who knew my day would end with snorin'?
Through zm inflammation, I have found
The quest for buttons all around.

So here's to all who dare and seek,
In the dark, the future's bleak.
But laughter echoes in this plight,
As I tune in to endless night.

Embracing the Absence of Touch

Barbecue chips and soda pop,
Remote's not here? Time to stop!
Can I survive without a click?
Maybe it's just a brilliant trick.

The sofa laughs, it knows the tale,
How I searched and started to flail.
With arms outstretched, I climb up high,
To reach all cushions, give that a try!

Each spot reveals a snack attack,
Crumbs of joy along the track.
But in this game of hide and seek,
My heart knows 'touch' is all too weak.

So I embrace this nudged defect,
In every crease, new thoughts reflect.
What if the fun is in the chase?
Turn on the laughter, that's my place.

The Contemplative Clicker Chronicles

Once upon a time, it shined,
The clicker was my heart and mind.
Now lost, like sand beneath the waves,
My hands wander, busy like knaves.

Each button holds a mystery,
Why was I so blind, you see?
A treasure hunt, I've wandered through,
While daytime shows still mock my view.

A flick of the wrist, a final prayer,
"Remote control, are you hiding where?"
I dance with hope and endless jest,
To find the gem my heart knows best.

Laughter echoes in the void,
In this world, I'm quite enjoyed.
With each misstep in this grand race,
I find new joys in dust and space.

Finding Patterns in the Noise

What's that buzzing? Or perhaps a beep?
Finding sound bites, wake from sleep.
Patterns emerge in this dull haze,
While I'm lost in a dive of malaise.

With every hiccup and distant glitch,
Remote or ghost? Which is the hitch?
I navigate through phantom sounds,
As laughter's tune is what abounds.

Redundant channels in endless loops,
Mapping out through silly troops.
A cosmic dance of fate and wit,
Until I find that rascal bit!

So I laugh at all the waves,
In quest of joy, my spirit braves.
For in the chaos, there lies the clue,
That giggles hide when lost from view.

Emanations from an Ordinary Object

In the couch I lose my way,
Found a penny, come what may.
Beneath the cushions, magic lies,
But the remote? Just alibis.

Frantically I lift the throw,
Finding crumbs from long ago.
With every search, my patience thins,
Yet laughter echoes, where it begins.

Shadows play on the wall so bright,
In the chaos, there's delight.
Remote, a trickster on the prowl,
Stealing moments with a laugh and howl.

So I dance around the seat,
In this game of hide and seek.
What if one day I should find,
Enlightenment, of the remote kind!

The Lingering Click of Introspection

Click it once, but where's the show?
In this moment, thoughts can flow.
Every button hides a quest,
To find joy, I must invest.

Who knew this piece could make me ponder,
In its weight, I start to wonder.
Each channel crossed, a life I fake,
Clicks of life, for goodness' sake!

The static hum becomes my muse,
In remote's riddle, I can't refuse.
A snack or two will ease the pain,
While I search for sanity again.

In this room of animated air,
Will my wisdom find it there?
A click, a pause, the show unfolds,
In laughter's echo, life retold.

Dialogues with the Handheld

Oh dear device, where can you be?
I've called you friend, yet you ghost me.
Let's chat about this faulty quest,
In humor, dear remote, I jest.

We ponder like philosophers wise,
In a world of buttons and surprise.
Yet each flick, a question raised,
Of time and space, we're both amazed.

Lost in the realm of endless clicks,
With every show, a better fix.
Remote, por favor, don't play coy,
Help me find my channel of joy.

In a meeting of hand and screen,
The search recalls what might have been.
So let's embrace this game of fun,
For laughter, love, and light we run.

Enigmas at the Edge of Comfort

Comfort's zone, where cushions dwell,
Yet oh so far, remote's farewell!
A quest that sends my mind in whirl,
As laughter twirls and thoughts unfurl.

What is meaning in this lost delight?
To search by day, and roam by night.
Every nook, a possibility found,
Yet in the sounds, confusion is crowned.

Fumbling fingers, grains of sand,
Will I ever understand?
With every click, a chuckle grows,
In this jest, my journey flows.

So here I sit, in playful sweat,
Finding peace I won't forget.
Mysteries unfold, light on my face,
In this madcap chase, I find my place!

A Journey Through the Ether

In the couch's deep embrace, I dive,
Where crumbs and lost socks seem to thrive.
Chasing the magic of flickering lights,
Dancing with shadows on careless nights.

Remote, where art thou, my elusive friend?
Behind the cushions, do you ever bend?
A quest for laughter, a search for cheer,
In living room jungles, you disappear.

Is it hiding from me, in a game so sly?
Or does it plot with the cat, oh my!
Each creak of the floorboards echoes my plea,
As I ponder if my TV just wants to be free.

With every twist and turn, I seek your form,
A twisting adventure in chaos and norm.
Yet I'll find you again, in this cosmic chase,
And together we'll resume our majestic space.

The Remote's Silent Language

That little wand of fuzz and despair,
Whispers sweet nothings, it knows how to snare.
Button by button, my plans it does steal,
A game of mischief, an odd fun meal.

"Click here to laugh, click there to cry,"
It mocks my choices as shows drift by.
A secret language in each silent press,
Love-hate relationship, oh what a mess!

It hides from the dog, it dances with fate,
Each episode unfolding, oh isn't it great?
A tale of connection through channels we roam,
Finding joy in the chaos of my own home.

Yet one slip of the wrist sends me back far,
Needing a map just to find where you are.
But fear not, dear remote, we'll find a way,
Through the infinite power of binge-watching play.

Discovering the Unseen Pathways

Behind every couch, mysteries reside,
A treasure hunt full of whimsy and pride.
Fluffy pillows hide the truth ever bold,
Secrets of comfort and stories untold.

The hunt for the remote, oh what a jest,
At times it feels like some strange test.
Do the wires conspire with the hapless chair?
Or does the sofa giggle, caught in my affair?

In the land of the living, I take my stand,
Adventures await, all perfectly planned.
Navigating snacks and old magazines,
Searching for signals in strange little scenes.

A remote not in hand, but hope in my heart,
For every lost button is a brand new start.
I'll stumble through chaos, laughter my guide,
Because in this wild journey, fun will abide.

Intersecting Wishes and Reality

A fateful dance with cushions galore,
The remote plays hide and seek, I'm sure.
Each squeaky sound of a couch's old sigh,
Boasts of its ghosts as I desperately pry.

I wish upon stars for a magical sight,
To summon my remote with sheer delight.
Yet like a mirage, it disappears still,
Navigating chaos, what a quest, what a thrill!

A button's lost hope, a flicker of fun,
A dash in the dark, I race 'til I'm done.
Finding the funny in these tangled sways,
We laugh at the journey more than the ways.

So here's to our hunt, a whimsical spree,
Fumbling through memories, just my couch and me.
In the end, it's the laughter that brings us home,
Where even lost remotes are free to roam.

The Tapestry of Human Connection

In the sofa's depths, it stirs and hides,
Beneath the cushions, where chaos resides.
A quest for magic in a land of screens,
Yet there's laughter woven in all our routines.

One hand dives deep, the other takes notes,
As if we're sailing in seas of remote boats.
Sharing the treasure, a quest for the best,
Amidst snacks and banter, we humor the quest.

Inviting the Quiet into the Noise

With buttons around, chaos at bay,
We laugh at the silence that steals time away.
As worlds collide in our living room light,
Search for the click that feels just right.

A dog barks loudly, the cat takes a dive,
Who knew finding peace could be such a drive?
Yet in our folly, we frolic and cheer,
Turning lost moments to joy we hold dear.

The Breath Before the Next Show

A pause in the madness, TV sets glow,
With popcorn in hand, we prepare for the show.
Remote in one hand, a dream in our eyes,
We ponder life's questions, like who made this pie?

In laughter we ponder as we munch on snacks,
Reality's blur, through commercials and hacks.
So here's to the moments, both silly and grand,
In the quest for the remote, together we stand.

Fragments of Thought in the Click

Fingers dance wildly, a game of delight,
Every click echoes in the stillness of night.
In our search for the show that will steal our hearts,
We find silly moments that marble the arts.

Between bits and bytes, we laugh at our fate,
Like searching for wisdom, but ending up late.
Fragments of laughter, so fleeting, so bright,
Lost in the fun of the remote's playful fight.

The Mysterious Interlude of Stillness

In the couch's crevice, secrets hide,
The remote's lost journey, we cannot bide.
Pillows guard treasures, not meant to stray,
Yet laughter erupts as we search and play.

Under the cushions, a world we explore,
Distant lands of popcorn, and crumbs on the floor.
A game of hide and seek with a plastic friend,
Will we uncover the marvels that blend?

Shadows of mischief dance through the night,
A quest for the remote, oh what a sight!
With every lost moment, I chuckle and grin,
Who knew finding solace would bring such a win?

The stillness is charmed with giggles and glee,
A mission for treasure, just you and me.
In this realm of futility, we stand so bold,
Chasing after laughter, our hands turn to gold.

Channeling Thoughts and Dreams

In the realm of clicks and forgotten dreams,
A quest for the remote, or so it seems.
Couch cushions whisper tales of the past,
Of great battles fought, oh, how they last!

Remote control sorcery, magic supreme,
Wielding the power of a Netflix dream.
But where did it wander, my tiny stick friend?
In the realm of the lost, we'll search without end.

Dreams dance in pixels, a screen flickers bright,
But the remote is elusive, it shuns the light.
With every swipe and click, laughter ensues,
Our treasure hunt's magic is all we can use.

Thoughts drift like clouds past the living room's sky,
Guiding us forward, as time passes by.
In this patchwork of chaos, we find our delight,
Chasing echoes of joy in the soft evening light.

The Dimensions of an Escape

Through the fabric of space, the remote takes flight,
Into dimensions unseen, a curious sight.
Lost in the cosmos of cushions and fluff,
Each grasp reveals layers of mischief and stuff.

Across time traveling realms, we wander strange lands,
Searching for gadgets that slip through our hands.
With laughter our compass, we navigate well,
In this cosmic conundrum, we cast our spell.

Portal to joy lies in every click,
Yet the remote's antics have pulled quite the trick.
We twist and we turn, in this whimsical race,
Finding smiles in chaos, no need to keep pace.

Dimensions of laughter weave tapestries bright,
As absurdity reigns in our quest for delight.
A journey through fun, where bewilderment steers,
In search of the remote, we conquer our fears.

Transmissions Beyond the Couch

The couch is a spaceship, the remote's the crew,
Together we sail 'cross a galaxy new.
But oh, where's the contraption that helps us to fly?
Hidden in timelines where lost treasures lie.

Each cushion's a world bursting full of delight,
Transmissions of laughter echo into the night.
With snacks as our fuel, we soar through the air,
But the remote's adrift, and it doesn't seem fair.

Castaway adventures, we scour and seek,
The mission is grand, although we feel meek.
In flights of odd humor, we chase every sound,
In the wilds of the living room, joy can be found.

Beyond the horizons of channels unscrolled,
Our laughter is treasure, much more than gold.
When we finally find it, oh bliss will ensue,
In this comical mission, it's just me and you.

Transcendental Talks by the Remote

In the couch's deep abyss, it hides,
A tiny wand of magic slides.
With every click, a fate unfolds,
Philosophy in buttons bold.

I ponder deep in comfy chair,
Where did it go? I swear it's there!
A quest for peace in pixel light,
It laughs at me, oh what a sight!

If time and space can bend just right,
I'll summon it from endless night.
Yet here I sit, and here I stay,
A warrior lost in street's ballet.

Oh, buttons speak of life's demand,
Between the cushions, there it stands.
Entertained by silent screams,
The remote knows all my wild dreams.

The Color of Control in a Digital World

I grasp the wand with fervent might,
A palette rich in pixel light.
But often lost in channels wide,
Control slips smoother than a slide.

With every press, the colors dance,
From golden shows to a moody trance.
My fingers fly, a painter's quill,
Yet chaos reigns, and time stands still.

The guide is stocked with endless choice,
Yet somehow it stifles my voice.
Amid the pixels, I find it clear,
The colors clash, but I must steer.

In this wild ride of every hue,
I search for calm in all that's new.
With laughter ringing as I roam,
The remote becomes my digital home.

The Whispering Sea of Channels

Oh channel surf, a wavy sea,
What wisdom lies in all that glee?
With waves that crash and flickers fast,
A merry-go-round that's built to last.

In search of wisdom, lost in noise,
Between the clips and endless joys.
I fish for meaning in byte-sized bits,
While sitcoms play, and logic splits.

The landscape churns with vibrant tales,
As I ride on through storms and gales.
With laughter echoing from afar,
The channels twinkle like a star.

Yet all I want is just one show,
But choices bloom like weeds that grow.
So here I float in endless fun,
The remote's voice blends with the sun.

Threads of Serenity in a Buttoned Realm

In a kingdom ruled by buttons small,
A quest for peace amidst it all.
I navigate with gentle care,
In search of calm in pixel flare.

Amidst the chaos, calm I seek,
The quiet whispers in the geek.
A single press could change my fate,
Yet here I sit, just watch and wait.

A tapestry of shows unfolds,
Each thread a tale that life beholds.
From joy to tears, I weave the story,
In every click, I find my glory.

So here I dwell, a jester's mask,
In a world where buttons are my task.
With laughter and joy, I roam afar,
In this buttoned realm, I'll raise a bar.

Buttons, Choices, and the Passage of Time

In the couch abyss, I dive deep,
Each button whispers secrets to keep.
Should I pause the show or play it slow?
The remote's a wizard, but it's lost, oh no!

The universe twinkles, options abound,
Fast forward to laughter or rewind to frown.
Two clicks and a scroll, oh what a feat,
Life's pauses make snacks taste a bit sweet.

I ponder existence in a sitcom's glow,
Every choice a dream or a sitcom's blow.
As I flip channels, my fate's in a grip,
Is this enlightenment or just another blip?

Alas, I succumb to the sweet binge spree,
Time slips away like a ghost at sea.
Through buttons and banter, I aim to find,
The meaning of life in the reruns that bind.

Reflections on a Screened Reality

Pixels dance, a world so bright,
Yet here I sit, in dimmed twilight.
Reflections of wisdom on a flat face,
Did I just lose to my remote's race?

With screens that flicker, I ponder my fate,
Are these the moments I'll cherish, or hate?
I see my image, a funny distraction,
Caught in a loop of my own satisfaction.

Each click brings a chuckle, a gasp, or a tune,
Life's scripted laughter beneath the moon.
Trapped in this drama, what lesson to glean?
Is my purpose a sitcom, or just in between?

So I laugh at the stories, they pull on my heart,
And wonder what channel will play the best part.
In echoes of laughter, I begin to yearn,
For the truth in these tales, as I wait for my turn.

The Dilemma of Distraction

Sitting here battling, should I scroll or pause?
Each distraction a plan, what is my cause?
The show starts to chuckle, my brain gives a sigh,
But oh, what's that glitch? I can't just let it fly!

Remote in one hand, snacks in the other,
Will I conquer the couch, or let fate smother?
In the land of the binge, I begin to lose track,
The next episode's calling, no turning back!

Philosopher's plight with chips in a bowl,
Is this happiness or just remote control?
Rhythm of chaos in comedy's grace,
Tick tock, tick tock—my time's out of place.

Finally I pause, a moment to think,
Reflect on the humor, the choices, the link.
But the couch holds my heart and fluffy embrace,
In this merry distraction, I've found my own space.

When the Cosmos Aligns with a Button

When stars align, the remote's in view,
A celestial moment, what shall I do?
Click, click, giggle—what wonder awaits?
Even the universe chuckles at fate's rates!

In the cosmic comedy of endless streams,
Should I chase a plot, or just follow my dreams?
Each button whispers of galaxies far,
As I navigate space with a handy star.

A zany adventure or a mindless scroll,
Two choices collide, a cosmic control.
I laugh with the stars, they nod in delight,
As I pick popcorn over a starry fight.

So cheers to the moments, the laughs yet untold,
In a universe crazy, both gentle and bold.
Through space and through time, let this button fly,
With humor as my guide, I'm ready to try!

Ruminating on the Reach

In the depths of the sofa seat,
A hunt for the gadget can't be beat.
Coins and crumbs, they all collide,
But where's my remote? I cannot abide.

Perhaps it took a trip to the moon,
To frolic with asteroids, hum a tune.
Or did it vanish under a snack?
Oh remote, why do you not come back?

My dog looks at me with a sly grin,
As if he knows where my search begins.
But I suspect he's in on the joke,
That remote's an illusion, a mere hoax.

With weary eyes, I check the same places,
Under cushions, in dark, hidden spaces.
It's a quest so grand, yet one so futile,
Missing remote? Oh, what a trial!

The Buttoned-Up Search for Clarity

Buttoned up tight in my comfy chair,
I ask the universe—does it care?
With buttons that mock me, I sit here and sigh,
Where is my remote? Why oh why?

I see the TV glaring with glee,
Pretending to know what's next for me.
Yet without that device, I'm lost in the pit,
Wondering if this is really it.

Could it be hiding with my sanity?
Or plotting a revolt in a state of vanity?
Even the cat seems to know where it's been,
Rolling eyes in a game of sin.

I try to remember the last thing I watched,
But the mystery deepens—feels like I've botched.
In the land of cushions and misplaced bites,
Is this remote the lost treasure of nights?

Moments of Pause in a Digital Age

In this world so plugged, so fully wired,
My remote is lost, my patience expired.
Scrolling the channels feels like a test,
While looking for magic in the great couch nest.

Each moment of pause echoes the fun,
As I breathe and consider how far I've run.
Was it under the books? Or between my toes?
In this digital age, where did it go?

It's just a click, yet a quest for gold,
In a tale of struggle and legends bold.
To find this tiny box, oh the laughter set free,
Why's it akin to a mythic decree?

Lost in connections, yet never alone,
In every dark corner, I make my throne.
So here's to the chase as we shout and we cheer,
For life's little puzzles, let's give a big sneer!

Contemplations on the Couch's Edge

Perched on the edge of my plush domain,
I ponder this issue, driving me insane.
Where has it gone, this sly little thing?
Like a magician's trick, it's lost with a fling.

In the chaos of life, it's a simple request,
To pause and relax but can't find the best.
Did I leave it outside with the gnomes in the lawn?
Or did it decide to be an early dawn?

The cat gives a yawn, a stretch and a sigh,
As if he's the guardian, the wise little guy.
He twitches those ears, then turns with a tease,
While I beg for the comfort a button could seize.

So I search through my days for a sign or a clue,
In hopes that today, it will come into view.
For each moment of quiet deserves a great laugh,
A treasure that's lost isn't lost after all, it's my path!

Lost in the Pixelated Wilderness

In the jungle of cushions, I tumble and roll,
Chasing the magic, where's that little scroll?
My glasses are missing, my mind is a blur,
Remote runaway, oh, where did you stir?

The cat now is laughing, with the dog by its side,
A secret alliance, on this sofa they ride.
In between the snacks and the pile of clothes,
I search for the clicker, but no one knows!

Behind the great couch, a land full of crumbs,
The remote's on a quest, oh, here it comes!
Peeking from shadows, in the land of the lost,
But alas, what a journey, what a comical cost!

So I sit in confusion, my eyes all aglow,
Wishing for help, should I give it a throw?
The pixels are dancing, the show's about to start,
But first, I must find it—oh, dear little heart!

The Symbiosis of Thought and Action

In the realm of the living room, ideas collide,
As I ponder the universe, remote's where I hide.
Quite the conundrum, oh, where could it be?
Wrapped up in blankets? A mystery for me!

Thoughts whirl like laundry, in the dryer of mind,
While I scour the cushions, the remote's still unkind.
A dance of two players, both me and my chair,
In this odd symbiosis, who's really aware?

I wonder if gadgets just like to pretend,
That hiding and seeking is just 'til the end.
A philosophical puzzle, or pure lazy luck,
As I search for the remote, somehow, I'm stuck!

Epiphanies scatter like crumbs on my shirt,
As I sit here and ponder my accidental flirt.
With the depths of my sofa, I gamely partake,
In this quest for remote—oh, for comedy's sake!

Reflections in the Screen's Glow

The screen's light is flickering, a beacon of hope,
Yet my quest for the remote feels like a slippery slope.
Shadows are dancing all across the floor,
But the treacherous sofa hides treasures galore.

I lean over the edge, with a curious grin,
Feeling in places where crumbs should have been.
Perhaps it's a prank, my cat's clever scheme,
To hide all the remotes in a pixelated dream.

So I muse on existence beneath the couch wave,
With reflections of laughter, I feel like a knave.
Philosophizing deeply, should I calm this unrest?
Or simply embrace it, as a humorous jest?

As episodes beckon, to nature's delight,
I find my remote—oh, a glorious sight!
Adventures in pixel, among torn-up fluff,
I learned that my folly was just all in good fun!

Searching for the Lost Connection

Lost in a tangle of wires and dreams,
Is the remote a mirage, or so it seems?
Diving headfirst into the valley of couch,
Glistening remote, don't give me a grouch!

On a hunt for a button, my humor stays high,
As I yield to the chaos, and laugh till I cry.
Each swipe of the arm across fabric and fluff,
Is a dance of sheer madness—this searching is tough!

In the world of connections, like Wi-Fi that fades,
My quest for the remote has me lost in charades.
I swear it has feelings, it's playing a game,
'Til I find it again, nothing feels quite the same!

Yet it's laughter that saves me, through this wild chase,
For deep down inside, it's a beautiful place.
As the show finally starts, and I claim my own space,
I smile at the joy that my struggles embrace!

The Great Quest for Lost Control

In the couch's deep abyss, it hides,
A quest for comfort, hope abides.
With cushions tossed and snacks awry,
I ponder how this day did fly.

The dog is snoozing, blissfully sound,
While chaos reigns all around.
Remote? What's that? It's just a prank,
A treasure lost in the potato bank.

I seek a guide, perhaps a map,
To lead me through this furious gap.
With every lever, twist, and turn,
The flickering screen, my heart does yearn.

Alas! My quest takes quite some time,
Every second feels like a rhyme.
But laughter rings through all the stress,
Couch-potato life, I must confess.

Reflections in an Obscured Screen

An echo lives within the glare,
Of every movie, every spare.
Caught between reality and more,
The remote is lost, I'll just ignore.

Finger hovering over the power,
My brain, it spins like a spinning flower.
The cat now reigns with regal paws,
While I sit here, pondering the laws.

A battle fought without a foe,
In this grand game of peek-a-boo show.
Reflections dance, it's never clear,
What was that click? Was that a cheer?

With buttons pressed, my hope runs thin,
But oh, the joy lies deep within.
As laughter breaks the silence grand,
I embrace the chaos, just as planned.

Navigating the Channels of Existence

In a world of endless static waves,
I flip through lives the mind behaves.
This channel here, that one is gone,
But still my show must carry on.

Remote in hand, but where's the fun?
Hunting mutants? No! I'll just run.
Reality's channel seems so dim,
Yet here I sit – on a whimsical whim.

With comedy as my guiding light,
Fumbling through an endless night.
The sitcom plays, my heart does soar,
In search of laughs, I want nothing more.

As fate aligns the shows I see,
I chuckle at this irony.
For in this dance of chance and glee,
The remote's just part of me.

A Journey Through Plastic Buttons

Oh wondrous device of plastic gleam,
With buttons that smile like a meme.
I fumble through, for hours I stray,
In this wild game, I'm here to play.

Each click brings new adventures near,
A sitcom here or a drama sneer.
Yet in my grasp, the magic fades,
As I ponder on my grand charades.

They say it's simple, a child's delight,
But remote in hand, it's a thrilling fight.
With snacks arrayed and drinks on deck,
Take heed you'll need to keep in check.

And when at last I find my prize,
The night unfolds before my eyes.
With laughter spilling, fun must flow,
In the kingdom of buttons, I am the show.

Meditations on the Flickering Light

In shadows long, the couch does wait,
Lost in a search, I contemplate.
Where did it hide, that little device?
Perhaps it fled, seeking a new life.

The cat looks on, with knowing eyes,
Did it run off, or simply disguise?
A quest so grand, among the lost,
Finding joy, but at what cost?

Under cushions, it could be,
Will I find it, or set it free?
Each click of hope, a playful tease,
It's just a battle with the breeze.

Yet laughter bubbles through the strife,
Check the fridge? It's worth the life.
In every nook, a memory gleams,
For what is lost, there's always dreams.

Whispers of Comfort in the Void

The couch erupts in silent peace,
A void of hope, I seek release.
Where's that gadget, the tiny wand?
Perhaps it's having a little jaunt.

Remote, remote, where did you roam?
Do you miss the comfort of home?
In every crevice, I dig and probe,
In search of what I cannot behold.

Chocolate wrappers, old socks galore,
Is that laughter from the drawer?
The vacuum laughs, a friend in jest,
While I embark on this silly quest.

Yet amidst the dust and crumbs galore,
Joy is found in the quest for more.
With every turn and every glance,
Maybe the search is just a dance.

The Art of Seeking Solitude

In quiet corners, the phone may chime,
Yet here I dwell, with snack and rhyme.
Alone I sit, a loner's fate,
With no remote, shall I contemplate?

Oh, the irony, embracing gloom,
As the universe fills my room.
In solitude's grasp, I find my cheer,
A flicker of joy, despite the fear.

Remote-less hours, they call to me,
In every creak, a symphony.
With laughter light as I recline,
I grasp at joy like it's divine.

For life without it's a fun-filled art,
As I ponder where it might depart.
To seek within this space so still,
Is perhaps the thrill of my own will.

Unraveling the Mysteries of Leisure

Leisure reigns on this quiet floor,
With snacks by side, I can't ignore.
The quest for fun, I start anew,
Perhaps it waits, beneath the shoe.

Adventures grand in every room,
With playful antics, I silently zoom.
A remote, a prize, a trophy bright,
Yet finding joy makes everything right.

Under plush clouds, I make my plea,
Cushions spill secrets, if they agree.
With giggles blooming, I start to see,
The mystery's joy was always with me.

So I laugh in the face of remote-less blues,
Embracing the chaos, I peruse.
And in the end, what I'll uncover,
Is simply fun, and quite the wonder.

Between the Clicks Lies Discovery

Each click a treasure, hidden in the fluff,
In couch cushions deep, oh this hunt is tough.
Where did it wander, that rogue little toy?
With every press made, I find fleeting joy.

Under the sofa, I dive with grace,
In search of a gem that's fallen from space.
The dog chews a sock; what a curious sight,
Yet I'm still determined to find my delight.

Behind the fridge, a crumby old snack,
I never knew my love could lead to such wrack.
Digging through nonsense, the battle grows severe,
But I swear on this quest, I'll persevere!

At last, I unearth it; oh, what a win!
A remote reclaimed, let the channeling begin!
So here's to the laughter, the joy of the chase,
Between each click lies a cleverly hidden space.

Tracing the Vessel of Desire

In a cluttered realm of chaos and glee,
The remote vanishes, just like a spree.
I chase it through rooms, it darts with a grin,
Like a sly little fox, it's not letting me win.

Valiantly searching my chaotic nest,
Where socks and old bills go to take a rest.
Why must this gadget play hide-and-seek?
It's only a show; I just want to peek!

Under the cushions, it teases my heart,
"What did I watch?" that thought's a fine art.
Dictating my night like a conductor so wise,
Yet here I am fretting; oh, where is my prize?

Perseverance in hands like it's drawing a line,
Every tick of the clock feels like a bad sign.
Traced through the hours, I find my sweet quest,
In tracing desire, I've passed every test.

Seeking the Elusive Secret of Balance

In my home, there's a balance that's lost,
Remote control war, well, what's the cost?
With snacks piled high and chaos in sight,
Finding that button could spark pure delight.

I inch near the mountain of laundry so bold,
To conquer this beast, or so I've been told.
Underneath layers of fabric and fluff,
Awaits a small treasure; this isn't so tough!

But lo and behold, it's a TV block,
A mystical thing in a pile that I stock.
Finding that balance is hard as it seems,
But laughter erupts as I banish my screams.

At last, on a shelf, gleaming so bright,
The remote puts an end to my plight.
With joy in the air, I switch on the screen,
In seeking the secret, I dance like a queen.

A Quest for Focus in a Remote Land

In a realm of distractions, a fable unfolds,
The quest for my remote, the journey is bold.
Amidst all the chaos, the quest has begun,
With laughter and whimsy, let's have some fun!

"Where art thou, remote?" I call through the floor,
Echoes of silence come back with a roar.
Behind all the clutter, it winks with a tease,
This journey of mine is a whimsical breeze.

I rally my friends for a search party sure,
With snacks and distractions, it's never a chore.
Each "have you checked?" leads us further astray,
Yet laughter unites us; it brightens the day.

At last, in a cranny, with dirt and some crumbs,
The remote lies in wait, my heart beats like drums.
With focus regained and a hand on the prize,
I sit down to watch, oh the joy is no lie!

The Serendipity of Serene Choices

In the cushions deep, it hides,
A tiny quest, a tangled ride.
With snacks in hand, I search around,
For treasures lost, not yet found.

The cat looks on, amused and wise,
As I dive beneath, to my surprise!
A shoe, a toy, and crumbs galore,
But still no sight of that remote score!

Each nook explored, with hopeful glee,
Perhaps it's hiding, just to tease me.
In laughter and chaos, I do roam,
Amidst this journey, I feel at home.

A fleeting thought, what is its fate?
A cosmic prank or just my state?
Maybe the fun's in the wild chase,
Not the remote, but this silly space.

Weights of Decision in a Light Frame

Oh, to choose the channel, a noble plight,
Will it be action, or something light?
With snacks aligned and couch in sight,
One flick, and worlds will unite!

Yet here I stand, remote held tight,
A mountain of choices, none feel right.
Do I flip for laughs or hearts that break?
The weight of decisions makes my head ache!

A game of whiffs between my hands,
Laughing with fate, as tension expands.
Do I risk it all for the strange and new?
Or stick to reruns, the safe safety brew?

With every button, a journey unfolds,
In this tiny device, a universe holds.
Life's remote in my brightening gaze,
Makes me ponder in bewildering ways!

The Intersection of Intention and Convenience

To grab the remote, my mind constructs,
An intricate plan, with silly conducts.
Why can't it just stick to my side?
Instead, it plays the perfect hide!

From under the couch to the shelf so tall,
Each turn of the sofa, I hear its call.
A search party? Please, just one little thing,
Where is the bliss that this small box brings?

Intentions clash with convenience's game,
Caught in a spiral, it's quite insane!
When finally found, it seems to grin,
Just a tool for the chaos to begin.

Yet in the end, as I sit down with cheer,
The meandering journey was worth the sheer.
For laughter through struggles brings a glow,
And the best moments occur on this show!

Rewind and Reconsider

One quick press, and it's a rewind,
Back to that moment, my fate intertwined.
Did it slip through the cracks, or did I just lose?
A precision dance, now begins the ruse.

With every couch cushion, hope's vivid spark,
Yet nothing seems quite as I embark.
It teases and taunts, my digital twin,
But I've raised the stakes, let the games begin!

Around every corner, I'll search and I'll peek,
Under the cushions, oh-so-unique.
The saga of finding, it proves to be fun,
As I giggle aloud, feeling like I've won!

In this frantic chase, I find more than lost,
It's laughter and joy, without counting the cost.
So here's to the hunt, to the silly delight,
It's not just for shows; it's a whimsical fight!

The Art of Remote Control

In every couch, there's a secret game,
Where cushions hide treasures, oh what a shame!
I lift each pillow with hope anew,
But all I find is crumbs and goo.

The buttons glimmer with a promise so bright,
Yet in the chaos, they hide out of sight.
I swipe left and right, I twist and I turn,
Only to find my patience does burn.

Ah, the art of control, a maze of the mind,
As I chase those pixels, sweet freedom to find.
With laughter and sighs, I persist with my quest,
For in the end, it's the chase that's the best.

Each press is a gamble, a roll of the dice,
Will I land on a show that's worth my advice?
So here I remain, in this playful affair,
For the joy of the search is beyond all compare.

Where Do All the Buttons Go?

I have a remote that runs away,
It hides from my hand like a game we play.
Where do the buttons disappear at night?
Into the void, or perhaps just out of sight?

With each channel flipped, I think I'm quite sly,
But my remote has its plans, oh how it can fly!
It dashes through the sofa, it leaps from the shelf,
I ponder if it seeks a life of itself.

When tasked with a pause, it goes for a leap,
I'm left in the lurch, counting my sheep.
The clickers are ninjas, they dance 'round the room,
Leaving me puzzled, surrendering to gloom.

So I'll toast to the buttons, wherever they roam,
For this is their kingdom, and I'm just their gnome.
In this comedy caper, I'm the jester in line,
Searching for treasure while sipping on wine.

Echoes in the Sofa Abyss

Down in the depths of the sofa abyss,
Echoes of remotes take me to bliss.
With a rustle and rumble, I start my descent,
Hoping for comfort, my hopes are well-spent.

A remote is a phantom, it grants no reprieve,
Each flip of its buttons makes me believe.
Yet as I dig deeper, I find my own fate,
Lost in the cushions, now isn't this great?

What was once handy is nowhere in sight,
I'm left in suspense, oh what a plight!
A quest for the buttons, a treasure to seek,
But my journey suggests I might need a streak.

And still, I keep laughing, such folly we find,
In the textured labyrinth where comfort's aligned.
For though I may lose every battle and jest,
The chase for my remote is what I love best.

The Pursuit of Flickering Light

Chasing the flicker, oh what a delight,
I search for my remote in the dead of the night.
Each click brings hope, a potential reveal,
But all that I grasp is a sandwich's feel.

With giggles and grumbles, I scour my zone,
Did I leave it in the kitchen, or back by the phone?
It taunts me with silence, a true ninja win,
As I ponder on life and what could have been.

Through shadows I wander, like a true sleuth,
Each new discovery, a nugget of truth.
In the chaos of channels, I dance with delight,
For even lost gadgets can lead to insight.

Thus, I embrace this ridiculous chase,
For the laughter and joy find their rightful place.
In pursuit of the light and the flicks on my screen,
My heart finds its rhythm, in the quest for the keen.

Moments Between Consciousness and Void

In the cushions I dig, searching for gold,
But find only crumbs, half-eaten and old.
The universe waits, with a giggle, it seems,
As I ponder the void between all of my dreams.

Remote control lost, where could it be?
Did the cat take it, or's it got legs of its own?
The couch swallows things, like a mythical beast,
I unravel my thoughts, while others feast.

The Quest for Digital Solitude.

I embark on a quest, my mission in sight,
To find that device that vanished in the night.
The shows are all waiting, my snacks are all laid,
Yet here I remain, in a game tow'rd staid.

With cushions as fortresses, I wage a war,
Against the unseen, what's behind the door?
Remote, where are you? Like a ghost in a trance,
In a world full of pixels, I still must advance.

The Search for Meaning in the Mundane

In this labyrinth of life, where's the switch for the fun?
I sift through old wrappers, yet there's more to be done.
Every remote found is a triumph, I swear,
Leading me closer to the shows I don't share.

The laundry piles up, competing for space,
While dark thoughts creep in, about lost time and place.
I laugh at the chaos, it's all just a show,
As I sit on this throne of crumbs and woe.

Echoes of Isolation on the Couch

In echoes of laughter, I find my relief,
While the remote seems to mock my disbelief.
Where it's hiding, I cannot explain,
But please, take me back to TV again.

The right channel's out there, just out of my reach,
Like deep philosophical thoughts from a beach.
With popcorn in hand, I embrace this charade,
As the quest for the remote leads to better escapades.

Wandering the Spaces Between

In cushions deep where crumbs do wed,
I seek the device that once was my thread.
Will it appear on this bizarre quest,
Or vanish away like my last good rest?

The cat sits smug with her knowing stare,
Could she be the culprit? I must beware!
Under the sofa, behind the TV stand,
Each search seems futile, yet I still stand.

With snacks in tow and hopeful heart,
I crawl through the chaos, a work of art.
The universe laughs with each twist and turn,
But I shall not yield; there's much to learn.

So here's to the hunt, the mess, the plight,
For in playful searching, there's sheer delight.
One remote to rule, one remote to find,
In this cosmic comedy, I'm intertwined.

The Quest for Hidden Signals

I plunge into the depths of chaos and fluff,
Searching for signals that seem just too tough.
In the dark corners where odds stack high,
Is the remote hiding? Oh me, oh my!

My couch is a beast that swallows good stuff,
Phones and pens, yet it still feels rough.
With each awkward twist and a jaw-dropping bump,
I wrestle this monster, it's quite the slump.

With a laugh and a gasp, I stand up tall,
Check the pockets of jackets that lean on the wall.
Is this a remote or a lost time machine?
Certain it squirmed away like a dream.

In this zany chase, my sanity sways,
Through cushions and chaos on comic display.
The true prize awaits; I cannot relent,
A hero of couch and lost signals spent.

Navigating Life's Frequency

Lost in the waves of the living room bliss,
I tune in to frequencies that I can't dismiss.
Search high and low, it's a cosmic affair,
Is that a button? Or just empty air?

With cookies as bait and a cheeky grin,
I dance with the shadows, let the search begin.
The remote's like a ghost, always out of reach,
It hides in plain view as I try to breach.

I question the purpose of lazy leisure's throne,
Little do they know it's a vibrant zone.
Each click is a treasure, each pause a delight,
This journey through channels makes a curious sight.

So raise up your voice if you've lost your mate,
Together we'll laugh while we navigate.
In this humorous quest, under blankets we roam,
Finding the remote, we'll bring it back home.

In Search of Lost Channels

Once in a while, I journey afar,
In search of lost channels and my distant star.
Through buttons and gadgets, oh, what a spree,
Hold on tight while I search for the key!

There's a laugh from the fridge, a giggle from keys,
Coz every item seems to conspire with ease.
A squidgy old sock, a half-drunk canteen,
Is this my new beacon? This can't be routine!

With each failed attempt, I learn and adjust,
Perseverance and snacks are my way, my must.
The couch becomes psychic, predicting my plight,
It knows when I falter, it teases in spite.

But in this grand chase, with a wink and a jest,
Life's puzzles invite us, we must be the best.
So channel your joy as you coast through this maze,
For finding the fun is what truly pays.

Finding Balance in the Cable Jungle

In a tangle of wires, I roam,
Seeking the path to my cozy home.
The remotes are hiding, playing coy,
In this jungle, I search with joy.

Twisted HDMI, a foe so sly,
A cable monster that makes me cry.
Yet in this chaos, I find some glee,
A game of hide and seek with the TV.

With patience and humor, I fight the fight,
Dodging the chaos, aiming for light.
In the mess, I laugh, I dance, I sway,
Finding my remote, come what may.

As I conquer each button, I hear them tease,
"Good luck, my friend, we'll never cease."
But with each victory, my heart takes flight,
In this cable jungle, I see the light.

The Hidden Sanctuary of the Mind

Deep in my brain, a treasure hides,
A universe vast, where logic resides.
Yet amidst the stars, a remote appears,
Lost in the echoes of forgotten years.

With thoughts that drift like clouds above,
I ponder the channels, the shows I love.
In this sanctuary, I lose my track,
Chasing pixels, with no way back.

Mind like a maze, filled with twists,
Remembering buttons, I make a list.
But where's the sanctuary I sought to find?
It's just another remote—oh, the grind!

In equation and riddle, I search in vain,
Where the heck is that remote? Oh, the pain!
Amidst all the chaos, a chuckle I let go,
In this hidden chamber, I'll never know.

Remote Dreams and Digital Echoes

I dream of remotes that warp and sway,
In a pixelated world, I'd laugh and play.
Oh, pressing buttons like a conductor's hand,
Creating symphonies from my couch-land.

With digital echoes swirling about,
A voice from the screen begins to shout.
"Press me! Turn me! Find the tune!"
I just want to sit and watch the cartoon.

In dreams, my remote is sleek and bright,
Navigating channels, a pure delight.
But come morning sun, it's gone once more,
My quest for the remote becomes a chore.

I'll summon my courage, face my fate,
In dreams, I dance, while here I wait.
With a chuckle and grin, I know I must,
Find my remote—oh, how I trust!

Curiosity in a Sea of Buttons

A sea of buttons, shiny and round,
Each one offering mysteries unbound.
I poke and prod, with whimsy afloat,
In this vast ocean, I change the quote.

"Mute," "Channel up," "What's that?" I cry,
As the TV rebels, with a flicker and sigh.
My curiosity sails toward unknown shores,
Each press an adventure, a quest that adores.

Button by button, I search for the gem,
In this laughter-laden electronic hem.
With every click, a giggle I share,
In a sea of gadgets, nothing compares.

So here I stand, exploring the light,
With laughter and joy, I'll conquer the night.
For in this madness, I find my tune,
Curiosity thrives under the soft moon!

www.ingramcontent.com/pod-product-compliance
Lightning Source LLC
Chambersburg PA
CBHW071847160426
43209CB00003B/444